TWENTIETH CENTURY WORDSWORTH

TWENTIETH CENTURY WORDSWORTH

Margaret G. Barnes

JANUS PUBLISHING COMPANY
London, England

First published in Great Britain 1996
by Janus Publishing Company,
Edinburgh House, 19 Nassau Street,
London W1N 7RE

British Library Cataloguing-in-Publication Data.
A catalogue record for this book is available from the British Library

ISBN 1 85756 236 4

Cover design Linda Wade

Printed and bound in Great Britain by
Antony Rowe Ltd,
Chippenham, Wiltshire

CONTENTS

I

Prose Text on WORDSWORTH (1770–1850)

Foreword to the Prose

This paper was written originally in 1949. At that time the Sciences and Humanities in universities were quite separate fields of interest. Students pursued one or the other but never both, until after World War II when the Master of Balliol College, Oxford, resigned to open a university in the Midlands which required all students to read some combination of both. The practice has spread from there. I was fortunate to hear both fields discussed by my parents. Once, in the 1930s, I introduced a mention of Darwinian evolution at a seminar on English literature, but there was consternation on the face of the tutor, a scholar of the theology and philosophy in English literature.

My original paper pointed out similarities between Wordsworth and the forerunners of the present group of scientific philosophers, such as Alfred North Whitehead and Sir James Jeans. This put the English literature lecturers on their guard, for I got no help from any lecturer, critic or publisher in England, Canada or the USA. I put this study aside, thinking someone would deal with the subject in the next ten years or so. As far as I am aware, this has not happened.

In his prose works, Wordsworth says that in the future poets would write on scientific subjects which had become common knowledge. This also has not happened, although, as early as the 1930s, the Huxley brothers, Julian and Aldous, tried it without success. In the 1950s and 1960s I penned a few verses myself and had them published privately in 1986 as presentation copies for friends. They and the public were not then ready to accept such items. Now there is a gap in western thought, where orthodox religions are under a cloud among these same people, causing confusion, intolerance and cruelty, with no moral standards or respect for property. This the churches had provided in the nineteenth century.

This paper shows the development of my own reasoning on the expansion of Wordsworth's mind, and is followed by the verses, which I hope may lead people, more knowledgeable and really gifted, to fulfil Wordsworth's prophecy.

Julian Huxley's 1976 edition of his book *Religion without Revelation* has seen as far ahead as these present-day scientific philosophers in believing in the intelligence of the universe itself. He has also solved a problem of mine: I have often wondered how the chemical elements and their reaction to one another and other substances, could come into being without a creator; and how the delicate designs of crystals in metals and snowflakes could have stimulated us to appreciate beauty. Julian Huxley has written, 'The entire cosmos . . . consists of the same world-stough (William James' term for matter) which is both material and energy not restricted to material properties . . . the mind-like potentialities of the world-stough have been progressively intensified and actualised' (page 162); and again (page 163), 'If the self-creation of novelty is the basic wonder of the universe, the eliciting of mind from the potentialities of the world-stough . . . is the basic wonder of life.'

See Wordsworth's lines quoted at the end of my paper:

. . . and how exquisitely . . .
The external world is fitted to the Mind:
And the creation . . .
   . . . which they with blended might
Accomplish:

'They' are the world-stough and mind-like potentialities of Huxley, who quotes Wordsworth's 'Tintern Abbey' (lines 93–102):

> I have felt
> A presence that disturbs me with the joy
> Of elevated thoughts; a sense sublime
> Of something far more deeply interfused . . .

Huxley was unaware of Wordsworth's understanding of science, but sees '. . . the reality behind his thought that man's mind is a partner with matter.' He finishes the chapter on Evolutionary Humanism with the words, 'My faith is in the possibilities of man.'

 Wordsworth suggests the same, though less confidently,

> How exquisitely the individual Mind
> (And the progressive powers perhaps no less
> Of the whole species) to the external World
> Is fitted . . .

The end of the Preface to the Edition of 1814, written in 1797 or 1798, is a prayer:

> Descend prophetic Spirit . . .
>   . . . upon me bestow
> A gift of genuine insight . . .
>   . . . Dread Power!
>   . . . may my life
> Express the image of a better time,

More wise desires, and simpler manners;
                          . . . – so shall thy unfailing love
Guide, and support, and cheer me to the end!

TWENTIETH CENTURY WORDSWORTH

Wordsworth's knowledge of science such as it was in his day, gave him an understanding and appreciation of its values and dangers such as we see it 200 years later.

In the eighteenth century, philosophy embraced theology, psychology and science. Then science began to be regarded as a study in its own right. Astronomy, the oldest science, and geology were already pursued; Newton's force of gravity and Boyle's law on gases foreshadowed physics and chemistry; Locke and Berkeley were laying the foundations of future psychology. Then a group of scientists and others in Birmingham formed the Lunar Society (to aid travellers). Among its members were John Dalton, a chemist; Erasmus Darwin, a physician and biologist, and grandfather of Charles; Josiah Wedgwood, whose brother was a friend of Wordsworth; and, surprisingly, J M W Turner, an artist.

Educated at Hawkshead grammar school, Wordsworth was fortunate to have a headmaster, William Taylor, who taught mathematics and astronomy. He recognised the boy's ability and made a friend of him, preparing him for Cambridge, where he became senior wrangler. Wordsworth was so far ahead of his companions that he turned to the study of literature, especially poetry, which he began writing himself in the accepted rhymed couplet of the day. He used mathematics, geology and his intuitive insight into nature to escape from abstract thoughts and confusing emotions. After Cambridge he found that scientific facts were proof of his earlier insight, as Hinduism has done in our day. The whole physical universe of matter seems to have been, to him, an outward and visible sign of inward, immaterial, moral values.

In the poem 'The Simplon Pass', and again in 'The Prelude', such a passage occurs:

> ... The immeasurable height
> Of woods decaying, never to be decayed,
> The types and symbols of Eternity.
> (The Simplon Pass, lines 4–5, 19; The Prelude, Book VI,
> lines 624–5 only)

In the 'Ode to Duty' (1805) the laws of the universe, to which the stars are obedient, are a symbol for man's moral guidance:

> Thou dost preserve the stars from wrong,
> And the most ancient heavens, through Thee are fresh
> and strong.
>
> . . . .
>
> ... I myself commend
> Unto thy guidance from this hour ...
>
> . . . .
>
> The confidence of reason give;
> And in the light of truth thy Bondman let me live!
> (lines 55–56; 60–6i; 65–66)

In 'To the Moon (Rydal)', *Evening Voluntaries* No. 13, dated 1835, he seems to recall that Herschel discovered the planet Uranus in 1781.

> Worlds unthought of till the searching mind
> Of Science laid them open to mankind –

In this he reads:

The moral intimations of the sky, (lines 40–41, 48)

This theme is expanded in *The Excursion* Book IX, science revealing the immaterial quality of the universe, not God:

> ... Now shall our great Discoverers
> ... obtain ...
> From sense and reason less than these obtained
> Though far misled? ('these' were primitive peoples)
> lines 941–944)
> Enquire of ancient Wisdom; go, demand
> Of mighty Nature, if 'twas ever meant
> That we should prie far off yet be unraised; (astronomy)
> That we should pore, and dwindle as we pore. (biology)
> (lines 957–960)

Wordsworth was, however, not dogmatic; he is even agnostic:

> ... And if indeed there be
> An all-pervading Spirit, upon whom
> Our dark foundations rest ... (lines 968–970)

Is this a vague thought of Darwin's theory of evolution? He refers to this passage in 'Tintern Abbey':

> ... And I have felt
> A presence that disturbs me with the joy
> Of elevated thoughts; a sense sublime
> Of something far more deeply interfused,
> Whose dwelling is the light of setting suns,
> And the round ocean and the living air,
> And the blue sky, and in the mind of man:
> A motion and a spirit, that impels
> All thinking things, all objects of all thought,
> And rolls through all things. (lines 93–102)

This last is remarkable as linking our consciousness to the operations of the universe, as we are beginning to do. The idea is enlarged in the Preface to the 1814 edition of *The Excursion*:

> How exquisitely the individual Mind
> (And the progressive powers perhaps no less
> Of the whole species) to the external World
> Is fitted: and how exquisitely, too –
> Theme this but little heard of among men –
> The external World is fitted to the Mind;
> And the creation (by no lower name
> Can it be called) which they with blended might
> Accomplish:– this is our high argument.

In 1993 Paul Davies published *The Mind of God* (Penguin, p. 149, subsection 'The Mathematical Secret'). He writes: 'The mystery in all this is that human intellectual powers are presumably determined by biological evolution, and have absolutely no connection with doing science. Our brains have evolved in response to environmental pressures.'

To return to Wordsworth, in 1797 he had begged Josiah Wedgwood's brother to lend him a copy of Erasmus Darwin's *The Loves of the Plants* and *Zoonomia* (published in 1789 and 1794) 'for a very particular reason'. These embody a system of evolution similar to that of Erasmus' grandson Charles, and a detailed description of the reproductive system of both plants and animals, including man. Was Wordsworth's experience with Annette Vallon his 'very particular reason'? He also recognised in Darwin the elements of what we call psychology, treating it as a science like astronomy, physics and chemistry. In *The Excursion* he says, 'Ambitious spirits have solved the thinking principle.' (Book IV, lines 947–953).

8

Wordsworth used this new knowledge as a basis for his studies of childhood: 'We are Seven', 'Anecdote for Fathers', 'Alice Fell', 'Lucy Gray' and 'To H. C'. (Hartley Coleridge, six years old). Emotional problems are studied in a group of poems on the deserted mother and illegitimate child theme, an obsession based on his own experience with Annette Vallon: 'The Thorn', 'The Mad Mother', 'Her Eyes Were Wild', and especially 'Vaudracour and Julie', which parallels his own story. He had found Goodie Blake in Darwin's *Zoonomia*, which confirmed him in writing psychological studies.

He uses scientific terms in his discussion of poetry in the prefaces at the end of the Oxford edition of his poems, where he compares a stanza of 'The Babes in the Wood':

> These pretty babes with hand in hand
> Went wandering up and down;
> But never more they saw the Man
> Approaching from the Town.

with Dr. Johnson's parody:

> I put my hat upon my head
> And walked into the Strand,
> And there I saw another man
> Whose hat was in his hand.

and adds, 'yet the one stanza we admit is admirable, and the other as a fair example of the superlatively contemptible ... Why trouble yourself about the species till you have previously decided upon the genus? Why take pains to prove that an ape is not a Newton, when it is evident that he is not a man?' Wordsworth knew the work of Linnaeus, who had classified plants and animals. Further on, discussing what he calls vicious poetry and good, he wrote '... this advantage attends the good, that the individual, as well as the species survives from age to age, whereas, of the depraved, though the species be immortal, the individual quickly perishes.' Whether you agree with this or not is not the point: his use of scientific terms on abstract ideas does not alter the fact that he understood the meaning of these terms.

He uses scientific as well as literary language: one stumbles across names, direct mention of Archimedes (*The Excursion*, Book VIII, line 220), and Newton (*The Prelude*, Book III, lines 60–63):

> ... where the statue stood
> Of Newton ...
> The marble index of a mind for ever
> Voyaging through strange seas of Thought, alone.

or indirect in the suggestion of Linnaeus or Herschel. Among the *Itinerary Poems* of 1833 – when he was 63 years of age – there are two written as tributes to science and engineering.

> Desire we past illusions to recall?
> To reinstate wild Fancy, would we hide
> Truths whose thick veil Science has drawn aside?
> No, – let this Age, high as she may, instal
> In her esteem the thirst that wrought man's fall,
> The universe is infinitely wide;
> And conquering Reason, if self-glorified,
> Can nowhere move uncrossed by some new wall
> Or gulf of mystery, which thou alone,
> Imaginative Faith! canst overleap;
> In progress toward the fount of Love – the throne
> Of Power whose ministers the records keep
> Of periods fixed, and laws established, less
> Flesh to exalt than prove its nothingness. (No. 14)

Today the experts say that science is self-correcting. And
No. 42:

> STEAMBOATS, VIADUCTS, and RAILWAYS
> Motions and Means, on land and sea at war
> With old poetic feeling, not for this,
> Shall ye, by Poets even, be judged amiss!
> Nor shall your presence, howsoe'er it mar
> The loveliness of Nature, prove a bar
> To the Mind's gaining that prophetic sense
> Of future change, that point of vision, whence
> May be discovered what in soul ye are.
> In spite of all that beauty may disown
> In your harsh features, Nature doth embrace
> Her lawful offspring in Man's art; and Time,
> Pleased with your triumphs o'er his brother Space,
> Accepts from your bold hands the proffered crown
> Of hope, and smiles on you with cheer sublime.

In *The Excursion*, Book I, he actually mentions his
pleasure in mathematics:

> ... he lingered in the rudiments
> Of science, and among her simplest laws,
> His triangles ...
> Oft did he take delight
> To measure the altitude of some tall crag
> That is the eagle's birthplace, or some peak
> Familiar with forgotten years, ... (lines 270–276)

In the 'Immortality Ode' Wordsworth pays tribute to Erasmus Darwin in two brief references:

> ... Though inland far we be,
> Our Souls have sight of that immortal sea
> Which brought us hither, (lines 166–168)

– a suggestion of Darwin's theory of evolution as immortality out of the past. The second reference is the last two lines of the Ode:

> To me the meanest flower that blows can give
> Thoughts that do often lie too deep for tears.
> (lines 206–207)

Is it any wonder, realising that the reproductive system is the same in plants and animals as in man?

The fullest statement of his scientific philosophy is found in the last of the Duddon Sonnets, No. 34:

AFTER-THOUGHT

> I thought of Thee my partner and my guide,
> As being past away, – Vain sympathies!
> For, backward, Duddon, as I cast my eyes,
> I see what was, and is, and will abide;
> Still glides the Stream, and shall for ever glide;
> The Form remains, the Function never dies;
> While we, the brave, the mighty, and the wise,
> We Men, who in our morn of youth defied
> The elements, must vanish; – be it so!
> Enough, if something from our hands have power
> To live, and act, and serve the future hour;
> And if, as toward the silent tomb we go,
> Through love, through hope, and faith's transcendent
>   dower,
> We feel that we are greater than we know.

He was fascinated by forms and functions – today we call them morphology and physiology. And, paradoxically, our future life is what we leave behind us: progeny, work, influence.

The Duddon Sonnets are dated between 1806 and 1820. He wrote three lyrics to Mary among the Poems Founded upon the Affections, Nos. 15, 18, and 19. No. 19 laments the fact that he still doubts a life after death, and regrets that he has not Mary's serenity, adding, 'Peace settles where the intellect is meek.' (line 13). He knew his break with orthodox religion distressed Mary. Perhaps the last of the Duddon Sonnets is addressed to her, hoping to help her to understand his faith.

In *The Prelude*, Book VI, he values the study of mathematics and astronomy; and his knowledge of the geology of the Lake District, as shown in his *Guide to the Lakes*, is still used in guides issued in our day.

In *The Excursion*, Book VII, he wrote of biology as we do, i.e., there is no life without death:

>   . . . The vast Frame
> Of social nature changes evermore
> Her organs and her members, with decay
> Restless, and restless generation, powers
> And functions dying and producing at need, –
> And by this law the mighty whole subsists:
> With an ascent and progress in the main;
> (lines 999–1005)

In *The Excursion*, Book IX, the Wanderer, whom Wordsworth here calls the venerable Sage, meditates on eighteenth century metaphysical philosophy, using expressions such as 'an active principle' and 'from link to link', a reference to the classical Great Chain of Being; but he is clearly thinking of evolution:

> Spirit that knows no insulated spot,
> No chasm, no solitude; from link to link
> It circulates the Soul of all the worlds.
> This is the freedom of the universe;
> Unfolded still the more, more visible,

The more we know; and yet is reverenced least,
And least respected in the human Mind,
Its most apparent home. (lines 13–20)

In a letter Wordsworth speaks of The Bible of the Universe, hence natural law, not the Scriptures.

He even gave the Priest a confused speech hinting the same thought:

Oh! let thy Word prevail . . .
         . . . Spread the law,
As it is written in thy holy book,
Throughout all lands: . . .
Then, nor till then, shall persecution cease,
And cruel wars expire. (lines 638–650)

   . . . .

Alas! the nations who of yore received
These tidings, and in Christian temples meet
The sacred truths to acknowledge, linger still;
Preferring bonds and darkness to a state
Of holy freedom, by redeeming love
Proferred to all, while yet on earth detained. (lines
652–657)

Now our clergy are echoing this thought.

Wordsworth had dealt with this, not mentioning the Church or science, at the end of *The Prelude*, Book XIV:

This spiritual Love acts not nor can exist
Without imagination, which, in truth
Is but another name for absolute power
And clearest insight, amplitude of mind,
And reason in her most exalted mood. (lines 188–192)

   . . . .

Imagination having been our theme;
So also hath that intellectual Love,

For they are each in each, and cannot stand
Dividually. (lines 206–209)

Wordsworth's faith in science prompted him to make a prophecy not yet fulfilled. In the Preface to the 1800 edition of *Lyrical Ballads* he wrote: 'If the labours of the Men of Science should ever create any material revolution, direct or indirect, in our condition, and in the impressions we habitually receive, the poet will sleep no more then than at present. . . . The remotest discoveries of the Chemist, the Botanist, or Mineralogist will be as proper object of the Poet's art as any upon which it can be employed, if the time should ever come when these things should be familiar to us.' Aldous Huxley drew attention to this in 1959 – both he and his brother Sir Julian had published slim volumes of science poems in the 1930s.

There is a long poem, 'To Enterprise', No. XXXIV of *Poems of the Imagination*, published in 1822, in which Wordsworth expresses confidence in man's ability in the future; first, to fly – (aeroplanes?):

And hast thou not with triumph seen
How soaring Mortals glide between
Or through the clouds, and brave the light
With bolder than Icarian flight?

Next, in deep-sea observation – (a bathysphere?):

How they in bells of crystal, dive –
Where winds and waters cease to strive –
For no unholy visitings,
Among the monsters of the Deep;
And all the sad and precious things
Which there in ghostly silence sleep?

Then in ocean travel for speed and accurate timing –
(steamships?):

> Or adverse tides or currents headed,
> And breathless calms no longer dreaded,
> In never-slackening voyage go
> Straight as an arrow from the bow;
> And, slighting sails, and scorning oars,
> Keep faith with Time on distant shores?

He sees archaeology searching for secrets of the past in
desert lands:

> Egyptian tombs unlock their dead,
> Nile trembles at his fountain head;

And, exploration solving former unsuccessful attempts:

> Thou speak'st – and lo! the polar Seas
> Unbosom their last mysteries.

He predicts, as a result, satisfaction and joy for intellect
and art:

> – But oh! what transports, what sublime reward,
> Won from the world of mind, dost thou prepare
> For philosophic Sage; or high-souled Bard. (67–91)

Through all this interest in science, Wordsworth was
experimenting with his theory of poetic language and
style. He could see the plain language coming in Burns,
and mental studies in George Crabbe. He really did com-
bine the lyric style with the form of the ballad as found
in Percy's *Reliques* and others, in a way that Coleridge did
not fully understand except in 'The Ancient Mariner' –
hence the only poem of Coleridge's included in *Lyrical
Ballads*. They differed on the meaning of imagination and
fancy: to Wordsworth imagination is 'reason in her most

exalted mood' (as above), and 'We see into the life of things:' (see 'Tintern Abbey', included in *Poems of the Imagination*, line 49). Coleridge called his poem imagination, but it is fantasy, as is Kubla Khan; probably the drug-taking confused his mind on this point – 'He killed the bird that made the wind to blow.'

Wordsworth's use of simple, direct diction fulfilled a special purpose of his own. In a letter he says he deliberately wrote the poems in imitation of the chapbooks peddled among the poor, hoping to give them poems of a higher literary quality, in language familiar to the uneducated. One of the villagers who could read would gather a group for this purpose. As far as my own research went in London in the 1940s, only 'We are Seven' so appeared, the first time with this familiar title and the second time as 'The Little Maid and the Gentleman', both of which I bought.

Wordsworth's poems on child psychology, and those on emotional problems (deserted mothers, etc.) are experiments conducted on the open-minded, trial-and-error system of the scientific mind. He was in no sense a scientist himself, but definitely used the biologist's method to discover and prove what is known as romantic poetry as distinct from eighteenth century neo-classicism. As in biology, there were failures which have misled the critics, but also successes. *Lyrical Ballads* and other poems are true cross-breeding.

The Excursion is a series of discussions on all aspects of the growing industrialised society, woven into a great tapestry of western civilisation. He expresses the differing views of a Clergyman, a Priest, a Pastor, a Solitary, a Wanderer (who is a free-thinker), and himself. The subjects are economics, finance and trade; the education and health of children and the poor; labour relations and sociology;

historical background; science and religion; animal instinct and psychology of the human mind. He had enough of the eighteenth century in him to 'see life steadily and to see it whole'.

In the Preface to the Edition of 1814, Wordsworth says at the beginning that he had planned a long philosophical poem, 'The Recluse, containing views on Man, Nature and Society', in two parts. 'The first preparatory poem is biographical, and conducts the history of the Author's Mind.' This was eventually named 'The Prelude' by his wife Mary, and adopted by the editor for publication in 1850. The second part was published by Wordsworth in 1814 as *The Excursion* and includes his own views which he had intended to be a third part of 'The Recluse'. This he abandoned – one can only speculate on his reason for this decision. He recognised the good social work of the parish councils, and did not want to interfere with this aspect of the Church's influence. Charles Darwin refused to outline his philosophy, fearing to shock or alienate family or friends. And our true scientists today realise that all our twentieth century knowledge does not solve the mystery of the universe. Wordsworth probably faced the same obstacles.

To return to Wordsworth's views, it seems that his general outlook on the position of the human race in the universe is quite like ours today: in fact he was a humanist in the twentieth century sense, not just a pantheist, as he was considered in the past. He expresses thoughts similar to some found in A. N. Whitehead, Sir James Jeans, and the grandsons of T. H. Huxley, Sir Julian and Aldous Huxley. Now we have scientific philosophers like Stephen Hawking and Paul Davies who replace gods with the laws of the universe, as Wordsworth does, seeing them as everchanging and opening new fields of understanding.

Wordsworth also expresses optimism, in the 'Immortality Ode'. Having regretted 'the shades of the prison house', he adds:

> We will grieve not, rather find
> Strength in what remains behind; (lines 183–184)
>
> . . . .
>
> In the faith that looks through death,
> In years that bring the philosophic mind.
> (lines 189–190)

A similar gentle approach appeared in 1985. Jim Herrick's *Against the Faith – Some Deists, Sceptics and Atheists* points out (Penguin, page 234) that 'Although God has disappeared from the study of nature, science and religion seem not to be the opponents that some thought them to be in Darwin's day.' Our future sovereign has received consent from the Church to broaden his title to Defender of Faiths, which includes even humanists.

Paul Davies finishes *The Mind of God – Science and the Search for Ultimate Meaning* with a chapter headed 'The Mystery of the Universe', thus: 'The central theme that I have explored in this book is that through science we human beings are able to grasp at least some of nature's secrets. We have cracked the cosmic code . . . How we have become linked into this cosmic dimension is a mystery. Yet the linkage cannot be denied . . . Through conscious beings the universe has generated self-awareness.'

To conclude this paper, Wordsworth made poetry of this thought:

> How exquisitely the individual Mind
> (And the progressive powers perhaps no less
> Of the whole species) to the external World
> Is fitted – and how exquisitely, too –

The external World is fitted to the Mind;
And the creation (by no lower name
Can it be called) which they with blended might
Accomplish: – this is our high argument.

II

TELL WHAT THE EARTH IS SAYING
Foreword to the Verses

The idea for poems about science is to be found in the Preface to the 1800 edition of *Lyrical Ballads* by Wordsworth: 'If the labours of men of science should ever create any material revolution, direct or indirect, in our condition, and in the impressions which we habitually receive, the poet will sleep then no more than at present. . . . The remotest discoveries of the Chemist, the Botanist, or Mineralogist, will be as proper objects of the Poet's art as any upon which it can be employed, if the time should ever come when these things shall be familiar to us.'

That time came some decades ago, yet it is difficult to find more than a handful of poems dealing directly with scientific knowledge and its effect on the day-to-day thinking of the average person. These verses are merely an attempt to suggest what might be done by others, really gifted, to justify Wordsworth's astonishing suggestion 200 years before our time.

As Milton regretted, the loss of the beauties of classical legends in his day, so we can regret the now legendary beauties of orthodox religions. Many will feel with Thomas Hardy in his exquisite lyric, 'The Oxen', set to music by Benjamin Britten:

> So fair a fancy few would weave
> In these years! Yet, I, feel
> If someone said on Christmas Eve,

> Come, see the oxen kneel,
> . . . .
>
> I should go with him in the gloom
> Hoping it might be so.

The title of this group of verses is taken from George Eliot's *The Legend of Tubal,* who is credited with introducing to his people music in song, accompanied by the lyre. As he lay dying in old age, he heard Mother Earth calling to him, but he said music could no longer

> 'Tell what the earth is saying unto me:
> The secret is too great, I hear confusedly.'

Today we have learnt some of Earth's secrets, and must seek out the cosmic law for guidance and understanding.

SYMBOLISM – Trinity

In the beginning was – no beginning;
    only, the Becoming;
    no how, or whence, or when, or why;
    no conscious direction,
    or deliberate aim.

This Becoming, intelligence,
    called God the Father,
    brought forth the universe of substance
    and all it has become,
    from shapeless hydrogen to man –
    the entire lovely universe of matter,
    the offspring of the Father,
    called God the Son.

With conscious knowing, God the Spirit awoke
    from a long sleep of dreams,
    rising from mindless functions of matter –
    chemical reactions,
    electricity and magnetism,
    crystallisation,
    physiological processes,
    instinctive animal wisdom,
    emotional attractions,
and now – with conscious intellect –
    the great I AM.

Spirit become matter;
  matter again become spirit;
  Father, Son and Spirit,
  three in one and one in three.

No longer unconscious, without aim,
  purposeless,
  Man gropes his dim way,
  through doubt and ignorance,
  towards an unknown form of being.

Only by knowing whence he came,
  can he, with confidence see
  whither he is bound –
  from everlasting to everlasting,
  from eternity to eternity.

Only by reading the unconscious,
  his long strange ancestry,
  can he now guide
  the Becoming of the universe –
  his beautiful universe –
  with the sinless wisdom
  of his own unconscious past.

Only when his mind is
  'wedded to the universe' –
  this matchless universe –
  will such wisdom be his.

For he who has seen the universe,
  the Son, the body,
  has seen the Father, the intelligence,

And in his flesh has he seen God.

CREATIVITY

Motivating Power,
Soul of Mother Nature,
Urge within all living forms,
    surely it is you I hear:

'Seek and you shall find,
explore, invent;
knock and it shall be opened to you –
    But, exploit not, destroy not.

Strive to fathom my ways.
Co-operate with me.
    If not, you perish.

Defy my laws at your peril.

The Universe,
where time and space are not,
    always wins.'

ROOT AND STEM

Not long ago we watched man
    trying to discover
    how to use strength in materials.

He thought, and tested, and failed
    time after time;
    till at last he found
    that a flexible thread resists tension,
    that a hollow tube resists breaking.

So he tethered his horse with a rope,
    he moored his boat with a hawser,
    he slung his bridges on cables.

But he made his lamp posts hollow,
    and the grasping bars on his buses.

Then he looked at us,
    and opened his eyes in dismay:
    for a root grows a central cable
    to resist being pulled up by tension;
    and a stem grows a cylinder,
    that even the reed may not be broken
    by the wind.

And we laughed at man and his struggles,
  the kindly mirth of maturity
  watching the strivings of youth.

THE MARRIAGE OF CANA

The scribe's brows were knit.
    He copied a verse,
    then paused.

'No one will accept this plainness
    and simplicity,' he mused.

What of other religions,
    other scriptures?

They had survived for centuries;
    how could he give his infant scriptures
    longer life?

What was it in those other religions
    that held men?

And yes! The mythical,
    the supernatural;
    water in a jug poured out as milk
    made men into gods.

But he must disguise his in new fables:
    not a peasant supper, but –
    a rich man's wedding feast;
    not milk, but wine.

'Now,' he thought, 'my religion
    will be accepted;
    it rivals the old in wonder,
    and surpasses it in beauty and meaning.'

Alas! Scribe,
    the beauty and meaning are long since
    turned to mint and cummin and anise.

Only thy myth and wonder remain,
    deluding half mankind.

MORS JANUA VITAE

So says the lychgate motto,
Where death and sorrow pause,
Yet here's a truth of nature too,
A guide that overawes.

No life save out of death,
Corruption, chemical change,
Food for the vegetable world
Where beast and insect range.

Thus faith and science agree,
No conflict need disrupt.
Grant that the faithful, too, may know
That facts do not corrupt.

(St. Catherine's Church,
Gosfield, Essex)

THE LEAF (Photosynthesis)
My greenness is alone upon the earth.
   Nothing can do what I do.
   None knows my secret.

Even your brain, mighty man, cannot,
   with the help of the sun,
   make moss, or grass,
   or a cabbage, or an oak leaf.

Yet without such as these you would die.

Out of the earth,
   through root and stem,
   come salts in solution
   to fill my cells.

Then the light of the sun,
   (not warmth, nor substance, nor any touch;
   but mystic rays),
   makes crystals grow,
   stones into bread,
   water into wine.

Can the darkness in your mind
   not comprehend this light?
   Seek, noble man,
   seek and find my lonely law.

The Spirit whose consciousness you are
    wills it so,
    that you may know yourself powerful,
    virtuous and loving.

Then no longer need my greenness
    be alone upon the earth.

CRUCIFIED, DEAD AND BURIED

Here ends the lesson,
   for in Adam all die –
   how happily for you, young Nazarene.

If you could know this earth,
   the Man of Sorrows would cry out,
   with grief undreamt in life,
   'What have I done?'

They say you taught,
   'Sell that thou hast, and give.'
We buy, and buy, and buy, and keep our own:
   and this is Christianity to-day.

They say you taught,
   'Take no thought for the morrow,
   what you shall eat,
   neither what you shall put on.'
We cook, and eat, and dress,
   from dawn to midnight:
   and this is Christianity to-day.

They say you taught,
   'God is a Spirit.'
Our god is gold, success,
   a cluttered consciousness:
   and this is Christianity today.

So it is good to know that you died, too,
    young Nazarene.

Not even we could bear the thought
    if you should know what things are done
    in Jesus' name.

Sleep on, young Nazarene,
    as men have always slept,
    in calm unwittingness of those who come.

CELL DIVISION (Mitosis and Meiosis)

If you would see a miracle,
    get out a microscope
    and watch cells in division.
See how the stuff of life within the nucleus
    separates into short segments
    called chromosomes;
    each of these then splits lengthwise:
    an invisible pole at each end,
    some drift, or current,
    seems to say, 'Come'.

And, most strange sight!
    They go, when called,
    one from each chromosome to each pole,
    making two equal nuclei.

Next, the cell wall begins to fold mid-way;
    nearer and nearer, the two sides approach,
    until the constriction is complete.

Then final fission,
    two new cells,
    each half size,
    ready to grow full size.
                . . . .

But when two cells unite to form an offspring,
    watch thoughtful Nature jettison
    half the material from each parent nucleus,
    that the new third may not be overburdened
    with double bulk of stuff,
    yet carefully, accurately select
    sufficient genes to make a finished whole.

No chance haphazard here,
    but rational law to keep the race in proportion;
    for if by chance she forgets this law,
    the individual dies too surfeited.

What worth have fairy tales,
    mock human miracles,
    legends and myths compared with this?

For this is to be conceived of some spirit,
    yet many have desired to see the things you see,
    and have not seen them.

And Solomon, in all his glory, was not arrayed
    like one of these.

LEGUMINOSAE

When plants began to grow in their own right,
    did all draw nitrogen from the rich earth?

Did one, sensing that earth would then be poor,
    thus drained continuously,
    discover how to restore nitrogen to the thin soil
    then once more rich?

Leguminosae these are called,
    the peas, and beans and clovers,
    vetch, broom, laburnum,
    and a host of others.

Has then the common pea upon my plate
    more of intelligence and foresight
    than I can claim?

This is a thought that lies deep indeed.

FORGIVENESS
The law must be fulfilled,
   stern Nature:
   forgive you cannot.

To break the law is impossible;
   defy we may,
   yet suffer then due punishment
   for man's disobedience.

So always in spirit, too,
   the price must be paid
   in suffering or distortion:
   the law cannot waive.

Now man has invented forgiveness,
   'As we forgive them that trespass against us' –
   a gracious and lovely power,
   man's gift to you, stern Nature.

DRAGONFLY

Tiny intelligence,
    you rose above amoeba
    as your slim grace now soars
    over earth's waters,
    from reed to water flower.

Your insect families emerged
    in grass earthbound,
    from those which wriggle
    in water airless.

Dragonfly, your small brain
    cannot know man's thought –
    are you even aware of him?

What can you tell of calculus?
    of earthlore, organic or inorganic?
    of melody or rhyme?
    of abstractions on god and mammon?

Five hundred million years ago
    you ruled the earth as man does now.
    Five hundred million years from now
    will there be beings on earth
    as far beyond great man
    as he has outstripped you?

Are there, in those far ages,
    knowings and perceptions,
    even senses,
    of which he has no ken?

Those beings will look back
    and see proud man,
    in ignorance and imperceptiveness,
    as now you seem to him,
    Dragonfly.

GROPING
'With all thy mind' – I did, and
he dissolved into the cosmic order.
　　His own commandment slew him.

How can this be? Is he, perhaps,
'The all-pervading Spirit on whom
our dark foundations rest'? –

Symbol, metaphor, image for our
　　vestigial perceptions?

Can I, therefore, in this sense, still
worship him, in spirit and in truth,
　　with all my mind?

SECURITY

What have men to do with you,
    you gods of wood and stone,
    imaged by men's hands?

Or yet with you, oh Yahweh,
    imagined by men's minds in direst need,
    unbound by knowledge,
    to calm cold fear,
    comfort uncertainty?

The fish, the serpent and the ant,
    the bird, and the four-pawed beast
    know earth their home.

Man's home they also share,
    known and beloved far deeper:
    he studies their worth, and rejoices,
    that from such he came down the ages,
    of such he is by his birthright,
    to such he returns in due time.

Tranquil, he lives in his earth home,
    embraced by the whole wondrous system;
    nothing may uproot him from it,
    nothing may ever destroy him.

46

Always he has been in the universe,
    for a lifespan he knows this, is conscious;
    then again takes his place –
    with the physical elements, his body,
    with the energies and powers, his spirit.

Here is no 'mind's perturbation',
    no 'for ever and for ever farewell',
    no 'undiscover'd country from whose bourn
                        no traveller returns'.

He is the native, secure
    in the realms whence he came.

III

Appendix

With Foreword

APPENDIX

Foreword

In pursuing this study I have realised that Wordsworth knew a great many of the living forms of nature, and have made as comprehensive a list as I could, as I went through his poetry. He seems not to have travelled outside of Europe, but read extensively many travel books, perhaps trying to keep up with his brother John, who worked as master of a ship for the East India Company, though his special interest seems to have been the New World – the United States, the North West Passage in Canada and its explorers, and even Australia. As a result, there are several forms belonging to those areas which he could not have actually seen.

I have divided them into groups, with the number of specimens in each. Wordsworth once mentions reptiles, so he was aware of the new nineteenth century classification system; and five specimens appear elsewhere. The total, 219, has made the search worthwhile.

Herbaceous plants – 65

barley
bindweed
bramble (growing into a bush)
buttercup
campion, moss
carnation
celandine

corn
cuckoo flower
cowslip
crocus
daffodil
daisy (gowan, dialect)
dandelion
eglantine
eyebright
fern
forget-me-not
foxglove
gooseberry (called a bush when tall)
grape (vine, woody when grown)
grass
speargrass
harebell
hay
heather (sometimes a bush)
herb
honeysuckle
hyacinth
ivy (also woody when old)
jonquil
kingcup
leek
lichen
little robin
lily
lily of the valley
love-lies-bleeding (*amaranthus cordatus*)
marigold
marsh marigold
mint

moss
nightshade
oat
pansy
pea
periwinkle
pink
poppy
primrose
ragwort
reed
rush
snowdrop
speedwell
stonecrop
strawberry (sometimes called a bush)
thistle
milk thistle
thrift
thyme
turnip
vine
violet
wallflower

Trees and bushes – 41

acacia
alder
apple
ash
aspen
beech

birch
boxwood
broom
cherry
chestnut
citron
cypress
elder
elm
furze or gorse
hawthorn, red
hawthorn, white or may
hazel
heather (sometimes a plant)
hemlock
holly
juniper
larch
laurel
lime
magnolia
maple
sycamore maple
myrtle
oak
olive
palm
pine
plane
poplar
rose, briar
rose, hedge
thorn
willow

yew

ass
badger
bear
cat
kitten (young)
tabby cat (brindled, mottled or streaked grey or
   brown)
wild cat
chamois
deer
fawn (young)
hart (male)
hind (female)
roe (female)
roebuck (male)
spotted deer
dog
sheepdog
greyhound
hound
lurcher
dolphin (mammal)
fox
goat
kid (young)
wild goat
hare
buck (male)
leveret (young)

hedgehog
horse
mountain pony
palfrey (riding)
steed (war)
lamb
lion (Africa)
mole
mouse
newt (amphibian)
ostrich (Africa)
panther (leopard – Africa)
sea-horse (mythical)
sheep
ewe (female)
ram (male)
steer (castrated)
wether (male)
tiger (India)
toad
whale (mammal)
wolf
worm (not an insect)

Birds – 49

bittern
blackbird
blue cap (?dialect)
buzzard
cock
cockatoo (parrot – Australia)
cormorant

crow
cuckoo
dove
stock-dove
turtle-dove (wild)
duck
eagle
falcon
fieldfare
glead or glede
gull or sea-mew
hawk
dorhawk
heron
jay
kite
lark
skylark
wood-lark
linnet
magpie
mocking bird (USA)
muccawiss (USA)
nightingale
osprey
ostrich (Africa – flightless)
owl
paradise, bird of
parrot
non-pareil parrot (Australia)
plover
raven
robin or redbreast
rook

sandpiper
sparrow
stonechat
swallow
thrush
vulture
whip-poor-will (North America – name imitative of
   call)
wren

Insects – 11

bee
beetle
butterfly
caterpillar
cricket
fly
grasshopper
moth
snail
spider
wasp

Fish – 4

goldfish
silver-fish
herring
trout

lizard (with limbs)
serpent
slow-worm
snake
viper (poisonous)

Finally there is *homo sapiens* called (I think, by Aldous Huxley) 'the enigma, an animal with a brain'. As most animals have a brain, Wordsworth used a better expression, 'the thinking principle'. We are still our own deepest mystery and most challenging problem.

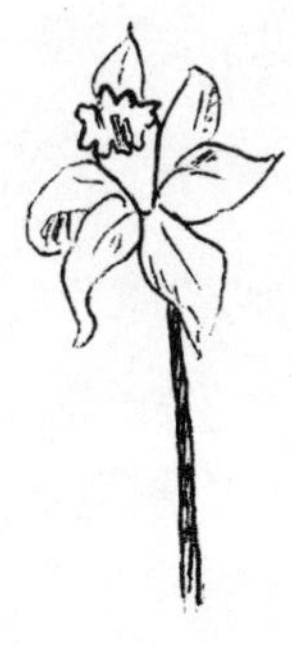